Explore the Solar System

Saturn
and
Uranus

WORLD
BOOK

a Scott Fetzer company
Chicago
www.worldbookonline.com

World Book, Inc.
233 N. Michigan Avenue
Chicago, IL 60601
U.S.A.

For information about other World Book publications, visit our Web site at **http://www.worldbookonline.com** or call **1-800-WORLDBK (967-5325)**.

For information about sales to schools and libraries, call **1-800-975-3250 (United States)**, or **1-800-837-5365 (Canada)**.

Library of Congress Cataloging-in-Publication Data
Saturn and Uranus.
     p. cm. -- (Explore the solar system)
   Summary: "An introduction to Saturn and Uranus for primary and intermediate grade students with information about their features and exploration. Includes charts and diagrams, a list of highlights for each chapter, fun facts, glossary, resource list, and index" -- Provided by publisher.
   Includes index.
   ISBN: 978-0-7166-9535-6
   1. Saturn (Planet)--Juvenile literature. 2. Uranus (Planet)--Juvenile literature. 3. Solar system--Juvenile literature. I. World Book, Inc.
   QB671.S234 2010
   523.46--dc22
                          2009029417

ISBN 978-0-7166-9533-2 (set)

Printed in China by Leo Paper Products Ltd.,
  Heshan, Guangdong
1st printing August 2010

Picture Acknowledgments:
Cover front: NASA/JPL/Space Science Institute; © Mark Garlick, Photo Researchers; Cover back: NASA/JPL-Caltech/UCLA.

© The Ancient Art & Architecture Collection 55; © Calvin J. Hamilton 11, 41; © A. Tayfun Oner from Calvin Hamilton 51; © Mary Evans Picture Library/The Image Works; JPL 32; NASA 13, 14, 22, 26, 27, 30, 43, 44, 53, 59; NASA/Cassini Imaging Team 25; NASA/ESA 18, 45; NASA/ESA/Cassini 33; NASA/JPL 52, 57; NASA/JPL-Caltech/Keck 20; NASA/JPL/Space Science Institute 8, 25; NASA/JPL/University of Iowa 15; © Mark Garlick/Photo Researchers 38; © Shutterstock 16, 46.

WORLD BOOK illustrations by Steve Karp 4. 34; WORLD BOOK illustrations by Paul Perreault, 7, 19, 37, 49.

Astronomers use different kinds of photos to learn about such objects in space as planets. Many photos show an object's natural color. Other photos use false colors. Some false-color images show types of light the human eye cannot normally see. Others have colors that were changed to highlight important features. When appropriate, the captions in this book state whether a photo uses natural or false color.

Staff
Executive Committee
Vice President and Chief Financial Officer: Donald D. Keller
Vice President and Editor in Chief: Paul A. Kobasa
Vice President, Licensing & Business Development: Richard Flower
Chief Technology Officer: Tim Hardy
Managing Director, International: Benjamin Hinton
Director, Human Resources: Bev Ecker

Editorial:
Associate Director, Supplementary Publications: Scott Thomas
Managing Editor, Supplementary Publications: Barbara A. Mayes
Senior Editor, Supplementary Publications: Kristina A. Vaicikonis
Manager, Research, Supplementary Publications: Cheryl Graham
Manager, Contracts & Compliance (Rights & Permissions): Loranne K. Shields
Editor: Michael DuRoss
Writer: Robert N. Knight
Indexer: David Pofelski

Graphics and Design:
Manager: Tom Evans
Coordinator, Design Development and Production: Brenda B. Tropinski
Contributing Photographs Editor: Carol Parden

Pre-Press and Manufacturing:
Director: Carma Fazio
Manufacturing Manager: Steven K. Hueppchen
Production/Technology Manager: Anne Fritzinger
Proofreader: Emilie Schrage

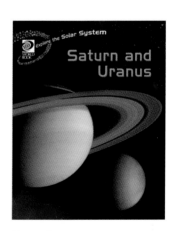

Cover image:
Saturn and Uranus (seen together in a combined image) are both gas giants, huge planets made mostly of gas and liquid.

Contents

If a word is printed in **bold letters that look like this,** that word's meaning is given in the glossary on pages 60-61.

Where Is Saturn?

Sun   Mercury Venus   Earth   Mars

Jupiter

Saturn is the sixth **planet** from
the sun. Saturn's distance from the
sun changes over time because the
planet follows an **elliptical** (oval-shaped)
orbit. On average, Saturn is about 891
million miles (1.43 billion kilometers) from
the sun. That is almost 10 times the
distance from the sun to Earth.

Saturn is one of four huge planets in
the **solar system** that **astronomers** call
the outer planets. The other outer planets
are Jupiter, Uranus *(YUR uh nuhs or
yu RAY nuhs)*, and Neptune.

Saturn

Saturn's location in the solar system
(Planets are shown to scale.)

Uranus   **Neptune**

Saturn's orbit is between the orbits of Jupiter and Uranus. The planet closest to Saturn is Jupiter. But Saturn and Jupiter are still very far apart. In fact, the orbits of Mercury, Venus, Earth, and Mars would fit between the orbits of Saturn and Jupiter.

Saturn is nearly twice as far from Earth as it is from Jupiter. That means that if a jet airplane could fly through space—at 500 miles (800 kilometers) per hour—it would take about 170 years for it to fly from Earth to Saturn.

Highlights

- Saturn is the sixth planet from the sun.
- On average, Saturn is about 891 million miles (1.43 billion kilometers) from the sun.
- Saturn's orbit is between the orbits of Jupiter and Uranus.

How Big Is Saturn?

Saturn is a giant, compared with most **planets** in the **solar system.** Only Jupiter is larger.

Saturn's **diameter** is 74,898 miles (120,536 kilometers) at its **equator.** Jupiter's diameter is only about 14,000 miles (22,500 kilometers) larger.

Fun Fact

Saturn is a giant in size; however, because it is made mostly of gas, it would actually float in water.

Highlights

- Saturn is the second largest planet in the solar system (only Jupiter is larger).
- Saturn's diameter is 74,898 miles (120,536 kilometers).
- The diameter of Saturn is nearly 10 times that of Earth's.
- The diameter of the sun is about 10 times that of Saturn's.

But Saturn is huge compared with Earth. Saturn's diameter is nearly 10 times that of Earth's. About 755 Earths would fit inside Saturn. Saturn is so large it can be seen from Earth without a telescope.

As large as Saturn is, however, it is much, much smaller than the sun. About 10 Saturns could line up across the width of the sun.

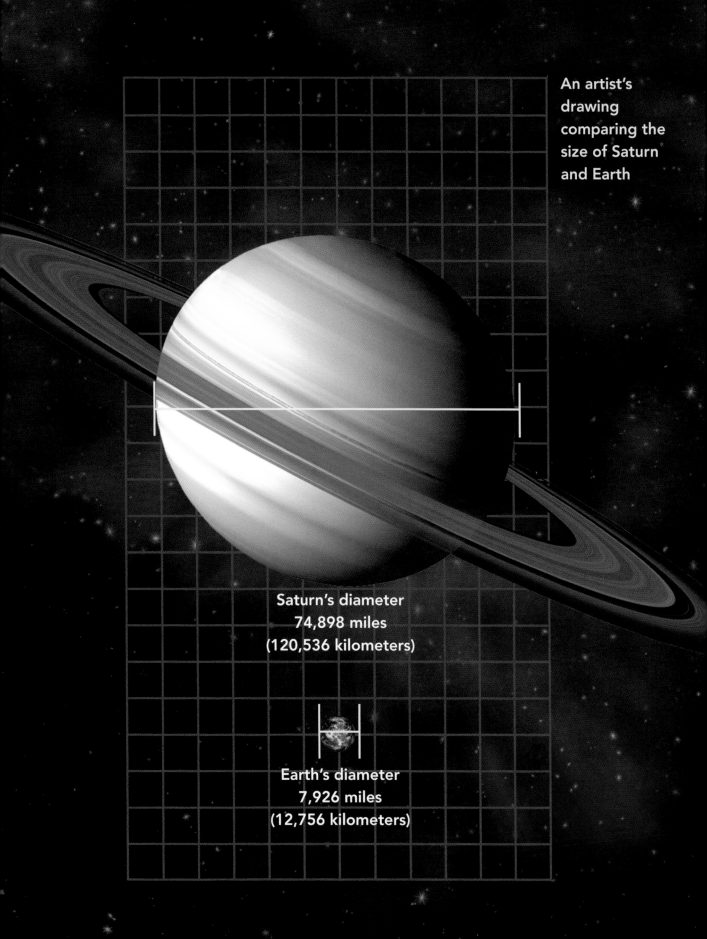

An artist's drawing comparing the size of Saturn and Earth

Saturn's diameter
74,898 miles
(120,536 kilometers)

Earth's diameter
7,926 miles
(12,756 kilometers)

What Does Saturn Look Like?

Many **astronomers** think Saturn is the most beautiful object in the **solar system.** In fact, the nickname of the **planet** is "the jewel of the solar system."

What sets Saturn apart from the other planets is its large, beautiful ring system. Jupiter, Uranus, and Neptune also have rings, but their rings are much fainter. People who enjoy watching the night sky only need a small telescope to view Saturn's majestic rings.

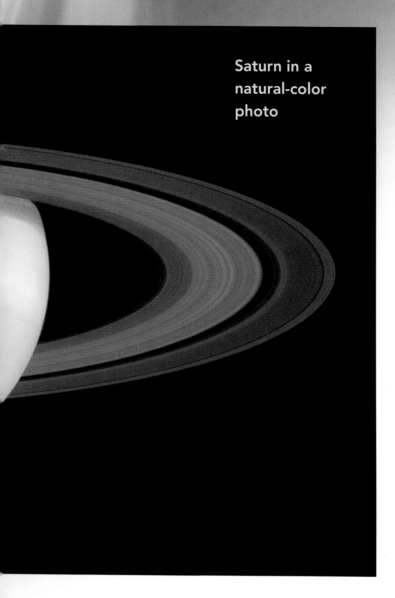

Saturn in a natural-color photo

Like its neighbor Jupiter, Saturn appears to be wrapped in bands. That is, photographs of Saturn show bands of different colors on the planet's cloud tops.

The various colors of the bands seem to be caused by differences in the temperature and *altitude* (height) of rising or falling air masses. Most of Saturn's clouds are yellowish in color. Clouds at higher altitudes appear lighter yellow, and clouds at lower altitudes appear darker yellow.

Highlights

- Saturn is nicknamed "the jewel of the solar system" because of its beautiful rings.
- The planet appears to be wrapped in bands, because it has layers of clouds of different colors.

What Is Saturn Made Of?

Scientists label the four largest **planets** in the **solar system** the **gas giants.** These planets are Jupiter, Saturn, Uranus, and Neptune. They have earned their label for good reason—all are huge planets that are made up mainly of gas and liquid.

Saturn does not have a hard surface like Earth's. Instead, it has an outer layer of gases, a liquid layer, and a **core.**

Saturn's outer layer is made up chiefly of **hydrogen** and **helium.** Farther down, the great weight of the outer layer forces the hydrogen and helium to become thick and syrup-like. Deeper still, the hydrogen is squeezed so hard that it turns into a liquid. Because this liquid acts like a metal in some ways, it is called liquid metallic hydrogen.

Highlights

- Saturn is one of the gas giant planets.
- It is made up chiefly of liquid and gas.
- Saturn's core is made of molten (melted) rock and iron.
- Saturn's outer layer of gas is made mostly of hydrogen and helium; below is a liquid layer made mostly of hydrogen.

Inside Saturn

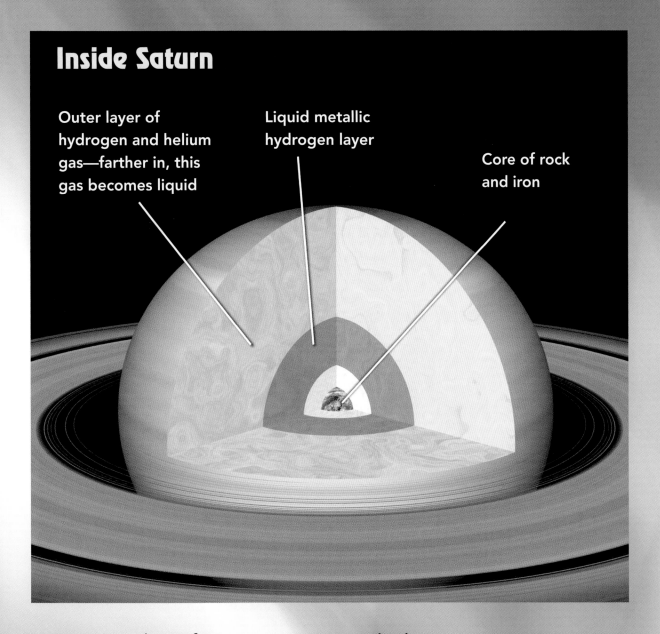

Outer layer of hydrogen and helium gas—farther in, this gas becomes liquid

Liquid metallic hydrogen layer

Core of rock and iron

For a number of reasons, scientists think Saturn has a hot, solid core. These reasons include the planet's shape, the way it spins, and the amount of pull its **gravity** has on other objects. The core is probably made of iron and other heavy elements.

What Is Saturn's Atmosphere Made Of?

On Saturn, the **atmosphere** consists mainly of helium and hydrogen. (The atmosphere is the layer of gases that surrounds a **planet.**) Farther down, however, these gases gradually thicken and become syrup-like. For this reason, scientists cannot pinpoint exactly where Saturn's atmosphere begins.

From Earth, Saturn's clouds appear yellowish. But in 2005, scientists made a suprising discovery about Saturn's sky. The unpiloted Cassini (ka SEE nee) spacecraft, launched by the United States National Aeronautics and Space Admin-istration (NASA), flew close to Saturn's northern region. Cassini sent back images of blue skies much like those on Earth.

Scientists think that the northern part of Saturn may not be covered by the yellow clouds found elsewhere. What can be seen instead is clear hydrogen "air." Do yellow clouds and blue sky shift around the planet from time to time? Scientists are trying to find the answer to this question.

Highlights

- Scientists do not know where Saturn's atmosphere begins, because farther down, the gases that surround the planet gradually become thicker and syrup-like.
- The northern part of Saturn has blue skies, but the rest of the planet is covered by yellow clouds.

The blue atmosphere of
Saturn's northern region
in a natural-color photo

What Is the Weather Like on Saturn?

Saturn is much colder than Earth. Temperatures at the cloud tops of Saturn's **atmosphere** average about −285 °F (−175 °C). The coldest temperatures on Earth—at the surface in Antarctica—are around −129 °F (−89 °C).

Highlights

- Saturn is much colder than Earth.
- Saturn is also windy, with storms that can reach speeds more than three times as fast as the most powerful tornadoes on Earth.
- Some of the storms on Saturn produce lightning.

The Dragon Storm (circled in a false-color photograph) in 2004 generated lightning 10,000 times as strong as lightning on Earth.

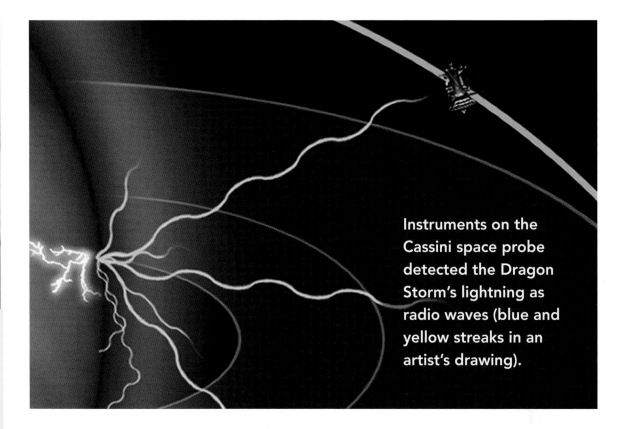

Instruments on the Cassini space probe detected the Dragon Storm's lightning as radio waves (blue and yellow streaks in an artist's drawing).

Temperatures in Saturn's interior are much warmer than those at the cloud tops. In fact, Saturn gives off about twice as much heat as it receives from the sun. Scientists believe some of this heat is created as Saturn *contracts* (shrinks) under the influence of its own **gravity.**

Saturn is a windy world. These winds are created by many spinning weather systems that look like storms on Earth. These storms may continue for months or even years. At the **equator,** wind speeds can reach up to 1,000 miles (1,600 kilometers) per hour. That's more than three times as fast as the most powerful tornadoes on Earth. Some of the storms also produce lightning.

How Does Saturn Compare with Earth?

Saturn and Earth have little in common besides being **planets** in the **solar system**. Saturn is a huge ball of gas and liquid. Earth is small by comparison and mostly solid. If the two planets were placed side by side, Saturn would dwarf Earth. Saturn is about 10 times as wide as Earth. You could fit about 755 Earths into Saturn.

Because Saturn is a gas ball, it has a lower **density** (the amount of matter in a given space) than Earth. Earth has the highest density of any planet in the solar system. Saturn has the lowest. As a result, a section of Earth would weigh eight times as much as an equal section of Saturn. Saturn's density is also less than that of liquid water. For this reason, Saturn would float—if it could fit into a container.

Highlights

- Saturn is much larger than Earth and has many more moons.
- Saturn has rings, but Earth does not.
- Saturn has less density than any other planet in the solar system.

How Do They Compare?

	Earth	Saturn
Size in diameter (at equator)	7,926 miles (12,756 kilometers)	74,898 miles (120,536 kilometers)
Average distance from sun	About 93 million miles (150 million kilometers)	About 891 million miles (1.4 billion kilometers)
Length of year (in Earth days)	365.25	10,759.22
Length of day (in Earth time)	24 hours	10 hours 33 minutes
What an object would weigh ...	If it weighed 100 pounds (45 kilograms) on Earth ...	... it would weigh about 90 pounds on Saturn, the equivalent of 41 kilograms on Earth.
Number of moons	1	At least 61 moons and many moonlets
Rings	No	Yes
Atmosphere	Nitrogen, oxygen, argon	Hydrogen, helium, methane, ammonia, ethane, water

Earth is much closer to the sun than Saturn is. On Earth, the sun appears as a huge glowing ball that lights our sky by day. From the cloud tops of distant Saturn, however, the sun would look more like a bright star in our night sky.

How Does Saturn Move Around the Sun?

Saturn's **orbit** around the sun is **elliptical** (oval-shaped). On average, the **planet** moves around the sun at a distance of about 891 million miles (1.4 billion kilometers).

Saturn's **year**—the time it takes to orbit the sun—equals about 29 ½ Earth years. Saturn is much farther from the sun than Earth is, so Saturn takes longer to travel around the sun.

Saturn **rotates** (spins) on its **axis** much faster than Earth does. A day on Saturn is only 10 hours and 33 minutes long.

Four of Saturn's moons (arrows) pass before the planet in a photo taken with the Hubble Space Telescope. The shadow of one of the moons is visible on the planet's surface (top, right).

The Orbit and Rotation of Saturn

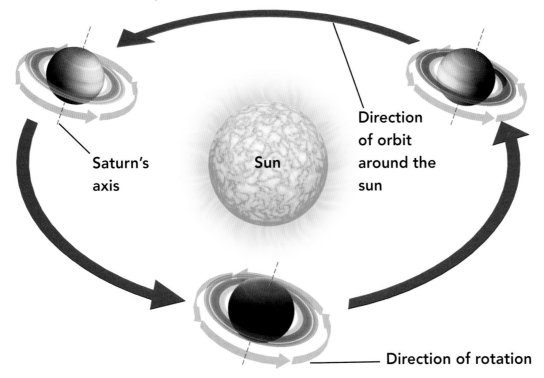

Saturn's axis

Sun

Direction of orbit around the sun

Direction of rotation

This is less than half as long as a day on Earth. Saturn rotates so fast that it flattens at its north and south poles and bulges at its **equator**. As a result, the **diameter** (distance across) at Saturn's equator is about 7,300 miles (11,800 kilometers) larger than its diameter from pole to pole. On Earth, those two diameters are almost the same.

Highlights

- Saturn's year is about 29 ½ Earth years long.
- Saturn's day is 10 hours and 33 minutes long.
- Saturn spins so fast as it moves around the sun that it bulges at its center.

What Are Saturn's Rings Made Of?

A spectacular system of rings surrounds Saturn at its **equator.** The rings are made mainly of pieces of ice. They range from dust-sized grains to chunks more than 10 feet (3 meters) in **diameter.** There are seven main rings and many thinner bands called ringlets. Scientists gave letters as names to the major ring bands. The rings were named in the order of their discovery. As a result, the names do not follow in alphabetical order.

Phoebe ring

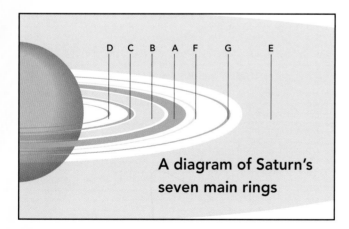

A diagram of Saturn's seven main rings

Highlights

- Saturn has seven main rings, many thinner bands called ringlets, and a giant ring that is the largest ring known to orbit a planet.
- The rings are made mostly of billions of particles of ice.

Saturn's main rings vary in width. The F ring is only about 20 to 300 miles (30 to 500 kilometers) wide. The Phoebe ring is about 16 million miles (25 million kilometers) wide.

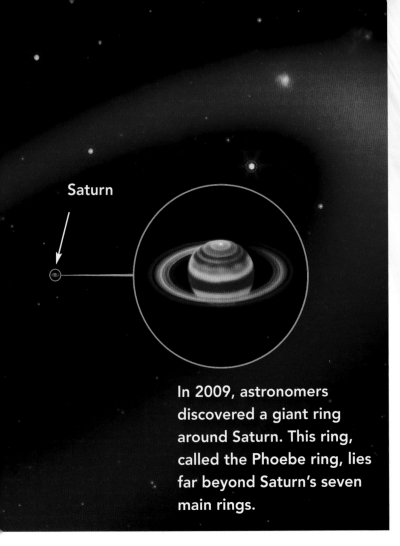

Saturn

In 2009, astronomers discovered a giant ring around Saturn. This ring, called the Phoebe ring, lies far beyond Saturn's seven main rings.

How did Saturn's rings form? Scientists think that a **moon** or other large object may have come too close to Saturn and broken apart. The breakup released billions of pieces that began orbiting Saturn. In time, the pieces formed into rings.

In 2009, astronomers found a nearly invisible ring of ice and dust particles around Saturn. That ring lies far away from the main rings, near Saturn's moon Phoebe. The Phoebe ring, as it is called, is the largest ring around a **planet** ever discovered.

In 2006, scientists found small gaps in the A ring. These gaps were apparently created by "moonlets" that are about 300 feet (100 meters) in diameter. The discovery supports the idea that the rings formed from a moon-sized body that broke apart.

Why Do Saturn's Rings Disappear?

If you viewed Saturn's rings night after night through a telescope, you might be surprised—or at least a bit puzzled. On one of those nights, you wouldn't be able to see the **planet's** rings at all. That's exactly what happened to Galileo (*GAL uh LAY oh* or *GAL uh LEE oh*), the Italian scientist who, in the 1600's, discovered what we now know to be the rings of Saturn.

While viewing Saturn, Galileo saw bulges along the sides of the planet. He thought they might be **moons**. Then, one night the "moons" were gone! Galileo never solved this mystery.

Fun Fact

Saturn was the farthest planet from Earth that ancient astronomers knew about.

Saturn and its rings in false-color photos

Saturn with its rings edge-on

Modern scientists know that the objects seen by Galileo were Saturn's rings. They also know why the rings disappeared. If Saturn is viewed when it is slightly tilted toward Earth (see the photo below), the rings are visible through a telescope.

Things are different when Saturn appears directly in line with Earth. If the rings are viewed edge-on (see photo on the opposite page), they seem to disappear into the blackness of space. Saturn's rings are edge-on to Earth about every 14 years. The last time the rings "disappeared" was in September 2009.

Highlights

- Italian astronomer Galileo was the first to see Saturn's rings "disappear."
- The rings seem to disappear about every 14 years, when Saturn is positioned directly in line with Earth and we are viewing the rings edge-on.

Saturn with its rings slightly tilted

How Many Moons Does Saturn Have?

On Earth, we are used to having one **moon** orbiting around us. Saturn, however, has at least 61 moons—though many of them are small. In addition, Saturn has millions of "moonlets" that are only about 300 feet (100 meters) in diameter. These moonlets orbit in Saturn's rings.

Titan (*TY tuhn*) is much larger than any of Saturn's other moons. Titan is 3,200 miles (5,150 kilometers) in **diameter.** By comparison, Earth's moon is about 2,160 miles (3,475 kilometers) in diameter.

Another of Saturn's large moons, Enceladus (*ehn SEHL uh duhs*), has an interesting trait— it is the shiniest object in the **solar system.** That is because its icy surface reflects most of the light it receives. In 2005, NASA's Cassini space **probe** discovered a thin **atmosphere** around Enceladus. Titan and Enceladus are the only moons of Saturn known to have an atmosphere.

Highlights

- Saturn has at least 61 moons and millions of small moonlets.
- Titan, with a diameter of 3,200 miles (5,150 kilometers), is Saturn's largest moon.
- Titan and another large moon, Enceladus, are the only moons of Saturn that have an atmosphere.

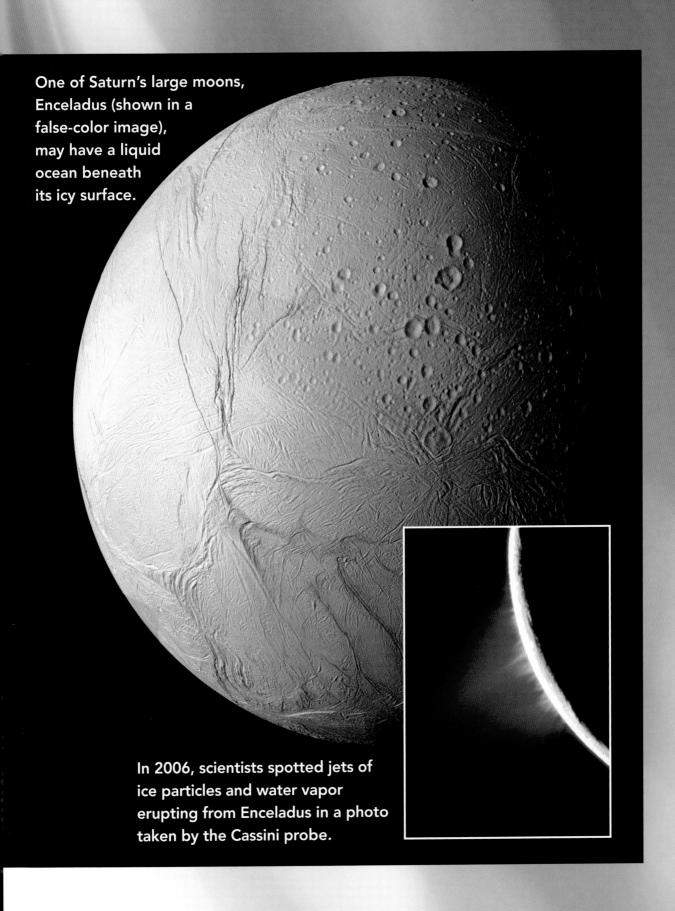

One of Saturn's large moons, Enceladus (shown in a false-color image), may have a liquid ocean beneath its icy surface.

In 2006, scientists spotted jets of ice particles and water vapor erupting from Enceladus in a photo taken by the Cassini probe.

What Is Special About Saturn's Moon Titan?

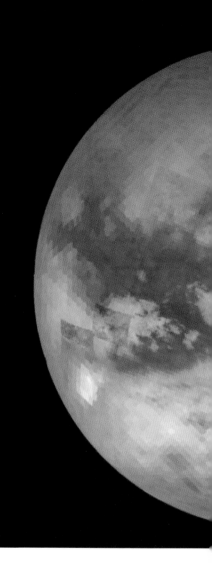

Titan is the second largest **moon** in the **solar system.** Only Jupiter's moon Ganymede (*GAN uh meed*) is larger. Titan is even bigger than the planet Mercury.

Unlike most other moons in the solar system, Titan has a thick, dense **atmosphere.** It is four times as dense as Earth's atmosphere at the surface. From space, Titan appears surrounded by a smoggy, reddish haze. That haze is made mostly of **nitrogen.** Clouds made of **methane** and ethane float above the moon's surface. Methane and ethane are chemical compounds that are found in natural gas. Many scientists think that Titan's atmosphere may resemble the atmosphere on Earth billions of years ago.

NASA's Cassini space **probe** revealed that Titan has seas that are filled with ethane and possibly methane. It also has mountains, sand dunes, and volcanoes that give off water and ammonia.

Titan and its dense, cloudy atmosphere in a false-color photograph

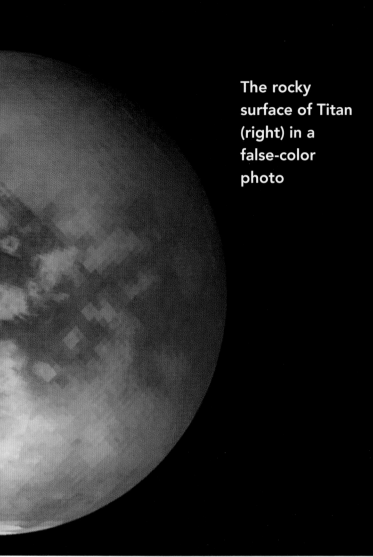

The rocky surface of Titan (right) in a false-color photo

In 2005, Cassini released the European Space Agency's Huygens *(HOY gehns)* probe above Titan. As it descended, Huygens gave scientists their first glimpse of Titan's surface. The probe also found that Titan is quite a noisy place. The noise is caused by winds. It sounded so loud because the thick atmosphere on the moon conducts sound waves better than thinner air does.

Highlights

- Titan is the second largest moon in the solar system. (Jupiter's moon Ganymede is the largest.)
- Titan has a thick, dense atmosphere.
- Titan also has a rocky, mountainous surface and seas that are filled with ethane and possibly methane.

How Did Saturn Get Its Name?

People have known about Saturn since ancient times. The planet—but not its rings—can be seen without a telescope.

Ancient Romans named the planet for their god of agriculture. In Roman **mythology,** Saturn was the father of Jupiter. The few myths about Saturn that we know of describe Saturn ruling over a golden age of happiness and plenty in the distant past. The word *Saturday* also comes from the name of this Roman god.

Highlights

- Ancient Romans named Saturn for their god of agriculture.
- In Roman mythology, Saturn was the father of Jupiter.
- The word *Saturday* comes from the name of Saturn.

A colored
engraving of
the Roman god
Saturn

Saturn is often pictured with a
sickle, a tool with a short, curved
blade on a handle that is used for
harvesting grain.

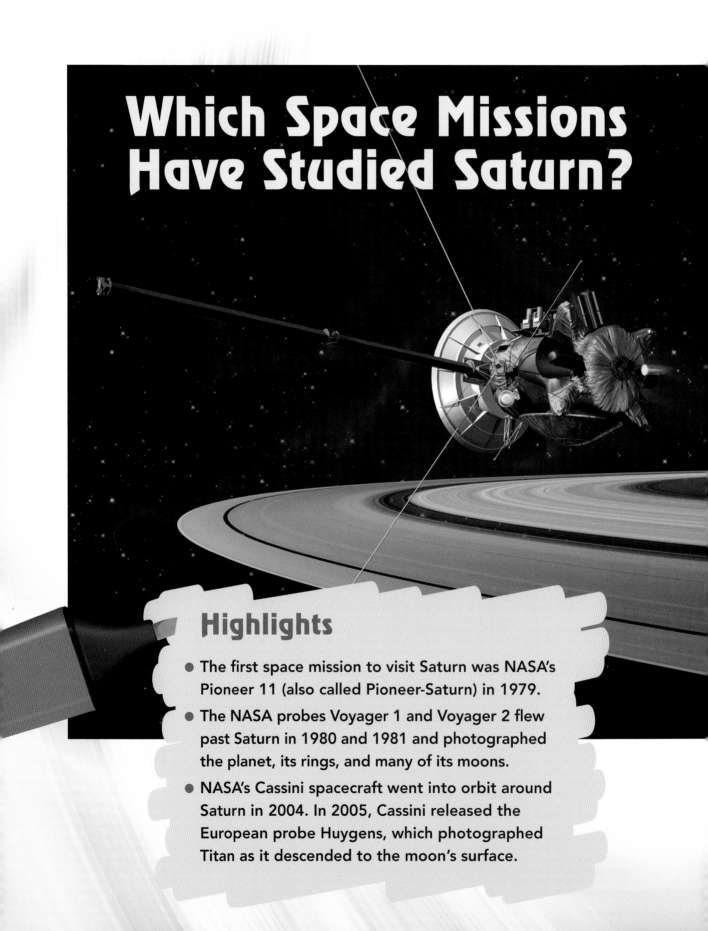

Which Space Missions Have Studied Saturn?

Highlights

- The first space mission to visit Saturn was NASA's Pioneer 11 (also called Pioneer-Saturn) in 1979.

- The NASA probes Voyager 1 and Voyager 2 flew past Saturn in 1980 and 1981 and photographed the planet, its rings, and many of its moons.

- NASA's Cassini spacecraft went into orbit around Saturn in 2004. In 2005, Cassini released the European probe Huygens, which photographed Titan as it descended to the moon's surface.

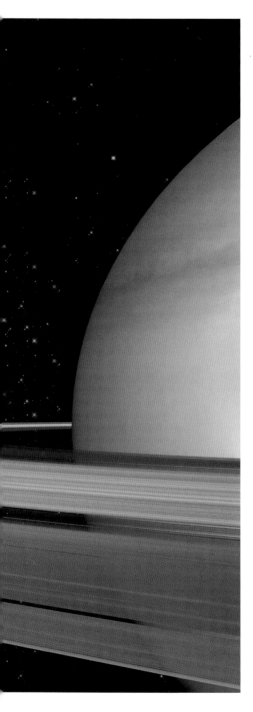

The Cassini probe orbits near Saturn and its rings in an artist's drawing.

Three NASA space missions have studied Saturn. The first, Pioneer 11 (also called Pioneer-Saturn), passed close to Saturn in 1979. It took the most detailed pictures of the **planet** seen at that time.

The twin space **probes** Voyager 1 and Voyager 2 were the next NASA spacecraft to fly by Saturn. Voyager 1 passed within 77,000 miles (124,000 kilometers) of Saturn's cloud tops in 1980. Voyager 2 swept within 63,000 miles (101,000 kilometers) of Saturn in 1981. The Voyager probes sent back amazing images of Saturn, its ring system, and many of the planet's **moons.**

NASA's Cassini spacecraft was launched in 1997 and went into **orbit** around Saturn in 2004. Cassini began to study the planet, its rings, and its moons. The spacecraft carried a probe called Huygens, built by the European Space Agency. Huygens parachuted through the atmosphere of Saturn's **moon** Titan and photographed the moon's surface as it descended.

Could There Be Life on Saturn or Its Moons?

Saturn is not a friendly place for living things. The **planet's** extreme temperatures and lack of **oxygen** make it impossible for human beings to survive there. Of course, we know little about the interior. But it seems unlikely that any part of the planet could support life.

The chances of finding life are greater on Saturn's **moon** Titan. It has a thick **atmosphere** and a solid surface like Earth's. Scientists think conditions are right on Titan for complex **organic** molecules to form. Such molecules are the building blocks of cells, the basic unit of all life. On the other hand, in 2005, the Huygens **probe** recorded a temperature of −291 °F (−179 °C) at its landing site on Titan. Could any form of life exist under such conditions?

Highlights

- Saturn has no hard surface, and its temperatures are so extreme that it is unlikely there could be life on the planet.

- But there could be life on some of Saturn's moons, such as Titan and Enceladus.

Seas or lakes of what scientists think might be liquid methane, or possibly ethane, appear in a photograph of Titan taken by Cassini.

Another moon of Saturn, Enceladus, may have the right conditions to support some type of life. In 2008, Cassini took samples from jets scientists had seen erupting from Enceladus's south pole. The probe confirmed that the jets contain water vapor and ice. The finding is evidence that liquid water exists below the moon's icy surface.

A photo taken by Cassini shows Titan behind Saturn's A and F rings, with the smaller moon Epimetheus circling above them.

Where Is Uranus?

Uranus (*YUR uh nuhs or yu RAY nuhs*) is the seventh **planet** from the sun. It is in the outer reaches of the **solar system.**

Sun   Mercury   Venus   Earth   Mars

Jupiter

Uranus is one of the outer planets in the solar system. The other outer planets are Jupiter, Saturn, and Neptune. The **orbit** of Uranus lies between the orbits of Saturn and Neptune.

Saturn is Uranus's closest neighbor in space. But the two planets are not really close. In fact, the orbits of Mercury, Venus, Earth, Mars, Jupiter, and Saturn could fit between the orbits of Saturn and Uranus.

Saturn

Uranus

Neptune

Uranus's location in the solar system (Planets are shown to scale.)

Uranus's distance from the sun changes over time because its orbit is slightly **elliptical** (oval-shaped). On average, Uranus is more than 19 times as far from the sun as Earth is.

Uranus is about 1.6 billion miles (2.6 billion kilometers) from Earth. That means that if a jet airplane could fly through space—at 500 miles (800 kilometers) per hour—it would take about 365 years to fly from Earth to Uranus.

Highlights

- Uranus is the seventh planet from the sun.
- It orbits, on average, about 1.8 billion miles (2.9 billion kilometers) from the sun.
- Uranus's orbit lies between the orbits of Saturn and Neptune.

How Big Is Uranus?

Uranus is the third largest **planet** in the **solar system.** Only Jupiter and Saturn are larger.

The **diameter** of Uranus at its **equator** is 31,763 miles (51,118 kilometers), or a little less than half the diameter of Saturn.

Fun Fact

Scientists think Uranus may have a rocky core about the size of Earth.

Highlights

- Uranus is the third largest planet in the solar system. (Only Jupiter and Saturn are larger.)
- The diameter of Uranus at its equator is 31,763 miles (51,118 kilometers). Earth's diameter is 7,926 miles (12,756 kilometers)—about four times as small.

Next to Earth, however, Uranus looks like a giant. Earth's diameter, at 7,926 miles (12,756 kilometers), is about four times smaller than that of Uranus. More than 60 Earths could fit into Uranus.

But compared with the sun, Uranus is very small. The diameter of the sun is about 864,000 miles (1.4 million kilometers). That means that more than 25 planets the size of Uranus could fit across the width of the sun.

An artist's drawing comparing the size of Uranus and Earth

Uranus's diameter
31,763 miles
(51,118 kilometers)

Earth's diameter
7,926 miles
(12,756 kilometers)

What Does Uranus Look Like?

Uranus is the farthest **planet** from the sun that can be seen without a telescope. In the night sky, Uranus appears as a faint point of light. Even when seen through a telescope, Uranus appears as a faint blue disk.

Astronauts sweeping by Uranus in a spaceship would see a smooth, blue-green ball. The entire planet is covered with pale blue-green clouds made up of tiny **methane** crystals. The crystals have formed out of the planet's **atmosphere.** The methane clouds absorb the red light in sunlight and allow the blue light to pass through, giving the planet its color.

Faint rings encircle Uranus, in an artist's drawing.

If the astronauts looked closely, they might also see Uranus's faint rings. Uranus's rings are narrow and dark or dusty and faint—not bright and flashy like Saturn's. Uranus's rings are easy to miss.

Like Saturn and Jupiter, Uranus has some bands and spots on its surface. But these markings are hard to see. The bands are made of different types of smog, a gas produced as sunlight breaks down methane gas. The spots are probably violently swirling masses of gas that resemble a hurricane.

Highlights

- Without a telescope, Uranus appears as a very faint point of light.
- From a closer distance, Uranus looks like a smooth, blue-green ball with dark rings.

What Is Uranus Made Of?

Like the other large **planets** in the outer reaches of the **solar system,** Uranus is made up largely of gas. Scientists believe that Uranus is a giant ball of gas and liquid. It does not have a solid outer surface, as Earth does.

Highlights

- Uranus is made up of gas and liquid with no solid surface.
- The planet's outer layer is made mostly of hydrogen and helium gas, topped with methane clouds.
- Below the gas may be a hot, liquid ocean of water and ammonia.
- At its center, Uranus may have a molten (melted) rocky core.

Like Saturn, Uranus has an outer layer made mostly of **hydrogen** and **helium** gas. The top of this layer consists of blue-green clouds formed of **methane** crystals. Deeper areas contain clouds of liquid water and **ammonia** ice. Deeper still, there may be a huge ocean made mostly of water and of ammonia that has *dissolved* (become liquid).

At the very center of Uranus may be a **molten** (melted) rocky **core** about the size of Earth. Scientists think the core of Uranus may be as hot as 12,600 °F (7,000 °C). Uranus produces less internal heat than the other **gas giants.** In fact, Uranus releases as much heat into space as it receives from the sun.

Inside Uranus

Outer layer
of hydrogen
and helium
gas

Ocean of liquid
water and ammonia

Core of
molten rock

What Is Uranus's Atmosphere Made Of?

Within Uranus's **atmosphere** of **hydrogen** and **helium** are clouds composed of **methane** ice crystals.

Uranus's atmosphere is not quite as big and, therefore, not quite as heavy as Saturn's. The atmosphere of Uranus is not heavy enough to cause the hydrogen at the bottom of the atmosphere to turn into a liquid.

However, the atmosphere on Uranus is heavy enough to affect the large body of water that makes up the middle section of the planet. On Earth, water would boil away at temperatures as high as those in Uranus's ocean. But the **pressure** of the atmosphere on Uranus prevents the water from reaching the boiling point and becoming a gas. So the ocean on Uranus remains a liquid.

Fun Fact

Although the atmosphere of Uranus is very cold, the interior of the planet is very hot—perhaps 4200 °F (2300 °C) in the ocean and 12,600 °F (7000 °C) in the rocky core.

The atmosphere of Uranus in a false-color photograph taken by the Hubble Space Telescope

Clearer areas of the atmosphere appear in blue.

Hazy areas of the atmosphere appear in yellow.

Highlights

- Uranus's atmosphere is made of hydrogen and helium with methane clouds.
- The planet's atmosphere is smaller and lighter than Saturn's.

What Is the Weather Like on Uranus?

The **atmosphere** on Uranus is far colder than even the atmosphere on Saturn. Scientists estimate a temperature of about –355 °F (–215 °C) in the cloud tops of Uranus. Uranus is far from the sun. In addition, it produces little internal heat, compared with the other **gas giants.**

Uranus's internal heat is too weak to warm the atmosphere. But it supplies enough energy to fuel violent storms. Sometimes the storms appear as dark spots on the surface. Winds howl around the southern half of Uranus at more than 450 miles (720 kilometers) per hour.

Clouds circle Uranus in a false-color photograph.

The bright orange areas represent fast-moving clouds.

Explore the Solar System

Another factor contributes to the weather on Uranus. The **axis** of a planet is usually *vertical* (up and down) when compared with a planet's **orbit** around the sun. But Uranus's axis is tilted far on its side. That means that the sun shines directly on the polar areas of Uranus as much as it does on the areas near the **equator.** On other planets, the equator gets more sunlight than the poles.

Uranus has four seasons—spring, summer, autumn, and winter. Each season lasts a little more than 20 Earth **years.**

A violent storm on Uranus appears as a dark spot (inset) in a photo taken with the Hubble Space Telescope.

Highlights

- The atmosphere of Uranus is very cold, though the interior of the planet is very hot.
- Uranus has violent storms and strong winds.
- Uranus has four seasons—spring, summer, autumn, and winter—that each last more than 20 Earth years.

How Does Uranus Compare with Earth?

Earth has very little in common with Uranus—or with any of the other **gas giants**. In size, Uranus dwarfs Earth. About 64 Earths could fit inside Uranus.

In addition, Earth is a mostly solid ball surrounded by a blanket of gases. Uranus is a ball of gas with no solid surface. No place on Earth experiences temperatures as cold as those found at the cloud tops of Uranus.

Perhaps the biggest difference between Earth and Uranus—and between Uranus and most other **planets**—is the tilt of Uranus's **axis**. (The axis is an imaginary line running through the center of a planet.) Uranus is tilted so far on its side that its axis lies nearly level with its path around the sun. Some scientists think that long ago a planet perhaps as large as Earth slammed into Uranus and knocked it onto its side. Others think that the pull of a moon that has since disappeared caused the tilt.

How Do They Compare?

	Earth	Uranus
Size in diameter (at equator)	7,926 miles (12,756 kilometers)	31,763 miles (51,118 kilometers)
Average distance from sun	About 93 million miles (150 million kilometers)	About 1.8 billion miles (2.9 billion kilometers)
Length of year (in Earth days)	365.25	30,685.4 (84 Earth years)
Length of day (in Earth time)	24 hours	17 hours 14 minutes
What an object would weigh ...	If it weighed 100 pounds (45 kilograms) on Earth ...	... it would weigh about 89 pounds on Uranus, the equivalent of about 40 kilograms on Earth.
Number of moons	1	At least 27
Rings	No	Yes
Atmosphere	Nitrogen, oxygen, argon	Hydrogen, helium, methane

Highlights

- Earth has a solid surface covered by an atmosphere made of gases. Uranus is a ball of gas and liquid with no solid surface.
- Uranus is much bigger than Earth.
- Earth has only one moon. Uranus has at least 27.

How Does Uranus Move Around the Sun?

Uranus is so far from the sun that it takes the **planet** a long time to complete its **orbit**. A **year** on Uranus—the time it takes to orbit the sun once—is about 84 Earth years.

The length of a **day** on Uranus is about 17 ¼ Earth hours. It takes Uranus that long to **rotate** (spin around) once and return to the same position in relation to the sun. However, much of Uranus's **atmosphere** rotates even faster. An area near the south pole rotates once every 14 hours.

Fun Fact

Because Uranus is tilted so far on its side, its seasons are very long. Each season is more than 20 years long!

Highlights

- One year on Uranus is about 84 Earth years.
- One day on Uranus is about 17 ¼ Earth hours.
- Uranus travels around the sun in a very different way from other planets because it is tilted much more than other planets are.

The Orbit and Rotation of Uranus

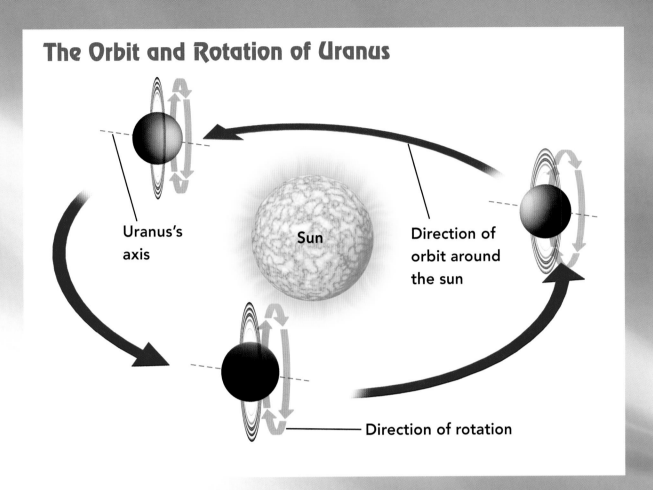

Uranus's axis

Sun

Direction of orbit around the sun

Direction of rotation

Uranus orbits the sun in a different way than other planets in the **solar system** do. Most of the planets rotate on their **axis** in the same direction in which they orbit the sun. Also, the axis of all the other planets in the solar system is only slightly tilted, either toward or away from the sun. As they rotate, they look like a spinning top.

However, Uranus is tilted so far on its side that it appears to travel in its orbit like a rolling ball instead of a spinning top.

What Are Uranus's Rings Made Of?

Like the other **gas giants** in the **solar system,** Uranus has a system of rings. Scientists have counted at least 10 rings circling the **equator** of the **planet.** Uranus's rings are rather dull and hard to see. Scientists think the rings are made of chunks of ice covered in a layer of **carbon.** The dark carbon absorbs more light than it reflects.

Because Uranus's **axis** is tilted sideways, the planet's equator encircles it from top to bottom. On other planets, the equator runs from side to side. Uranus's rings also run from top to bottom. Uranus looks different from Saturn, which wears its rings like a big, beautiful belt!

Highlights

- Uranus has at least 10 rings, but they are harder to see than Saturn's.
- Uranus's rings circle the planet from top to bottom, rather than from side to side as Saturn's do.
- Scientists first discovered Uranus's rings in 1977.

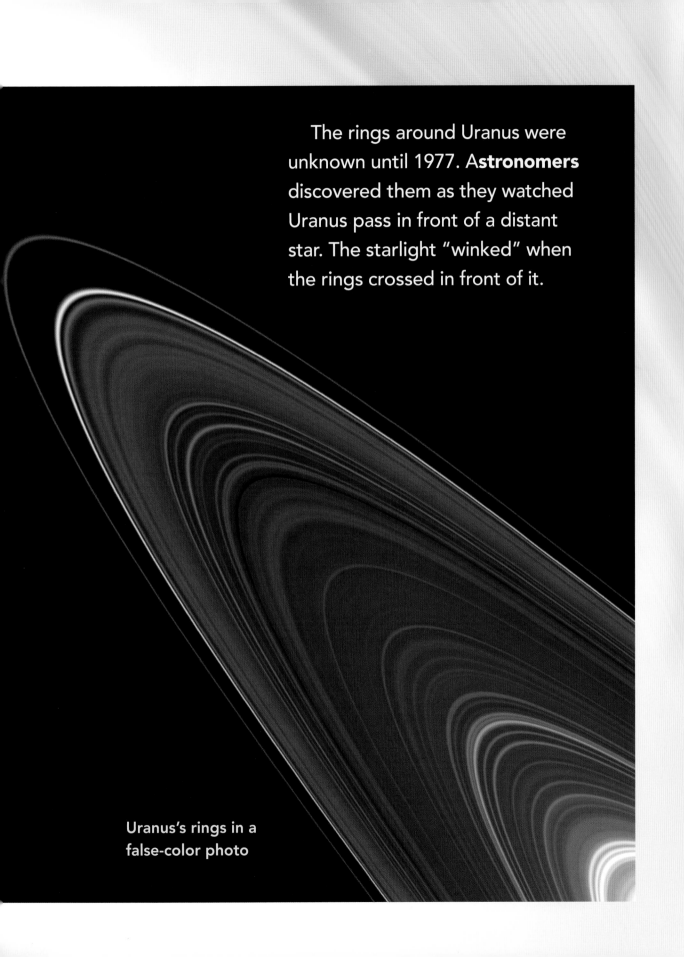

The rings around Uranus were unknown until 1977. **Astronomers** discovered them as they watched Uranus pass in front of a distant star. The starlight "winked" when the rings crossed in front of it.

Uranus's rings in a false-color photo

How Many Moons Does Uranus Have?

Uranus has at least 27 **moons,** but more will probably be discovered. Before Voyager 2 flew by Uranus in 1986, only 5 moons were known. Most of Uranus's moons are small, and their surfaces are marked with **craters.** Uranus has no giant moons like Saturn's Titan.

Uranus's moon Miranda (*mih RAN duh*) is one of the strangest objects in the **solar system.** It has three large, oddly shaped regions called ovoids. The outer areas of each ovoid look like a race track. They have parallel ridges and **canyons** wrapped around the center. Ridges and canyons crisscross one another in the center.

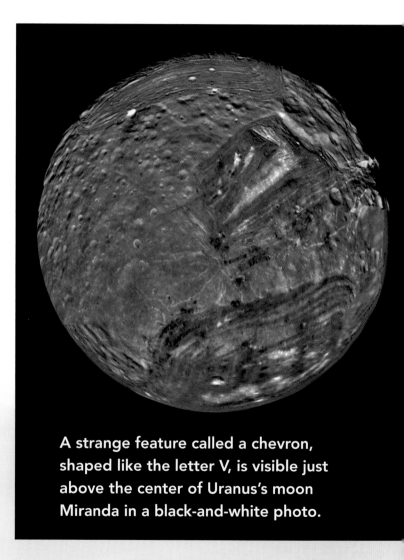

A strange feature called a chevron, shaped like the letter V, is visible just above the center of Uranus's moon Miranda in a black-and-white photo.

Oberon, Uranus's second largest moon, in a photo taken by Voyager 2

Some of the canyons are 12 times as deep as Earth's Grand Canyon. Another odd formation on Miranda is called the chevron (*SHEV ruhn*). It looks like a huge letter V.

Uranus's moons Cordelia (*kawr DEEL yuh*) and Ophelia (*uh FEEL yuh*) are known as **shepherd moons.** As they orbit the planet, their gravity keeps Uranus's outer ring within certain limits. They keep pieces of the ring from "wandering away."

How Did Uranus Get Its Name?

People in ancient times knew nothing about the **planet** Uranus. British **astronomer** William Herschel discovered it in 1781. Herschel named the planet Georgium Sidus, after the British King George III, but the name was not accepted by other astronomers. Later, a German astronomer suggested a name based on the *convention* (practice generally agreed upon) of naming planets after gods or goddesses from ancient Greek and Roman **mythology.** Eventually, the name of the first god of the sky in Greek and Roman mythology—Uranus—came to be accepted.

Highlights

- Uranus was first named Georgium Sidus by the British astronomer who discovered the planet, but other astronomers did not accept the name.

- Later, a German astronomer suggested the name Uranus, for the first god of the sky in Greek and Roman mythology. This name was accepted.

The names of Uranus's moons do not follow the same naming convention. The moons are not named for mythological gods. Instead, most are named for characters from the works of English playwright William Shakespeare. Among these characters are Oberon (*OH buh ron*) and Titania (*tih TAY nee uh*) from *A Midsummer Night's Dream*; Desdemona (*DEHZ duh MOH nuh*) from *Othello*; Ophelia from *Hamlet*; and Ariel and Caliban from *The Tempest*.

The god Uranus pictured in a Roman mosaic

Which Space Missions Have Studied Uranus?

The only space **probe** to study Uranus was NASA's Voyager 2. In 1986, Voyager 2 passed within 50,600 miles (80,000 kilometers) of Uranus. The probe had been launched from Earth in 1977 and had previously passed by Jupiter and Saturn.

Voyager 2 sent streams of data back to Earth. This information greatly expanded our knowledge about mysterious, distant Uranus. The probe detected a **magnetic field** around Uranus, which scientists had not known about before. It also estimated temperatures in Uranus's **atmosphere** and found that temperatures are about the same around the planet.

Voyager 2 found 10 previously unknown **moons** around Uranus—twice the number scientists had known about before. The probe also returned pictures of Miranda. The pictures revealed what an unusual object it is (see page 52 for more on Miranda). Voyager 2 also collected a vast amount of new information about Uranus's rings.

Highlights

- The only space probe to study Uranus was NASA's Voyager 2, launched in 1977.

- In 1985 and 1986, the probe discovered many more moons orbiting Uranus, as well as a magnetic field around the planet.

An artist's drawing of a Voyager probe

Could There Be Life on Uranus or Its Moons?

Uranus is not a very inviting place for human beings or other forms of life as we know it. Its **atmosphere** lacks oxygen, which human beings need to breathe. Some gases on Uranus are poisonous. Also, the temperature at the cloud tops on Uranus is piercingly cold.

Standing and sitting would be problems on Uranus. Because Uranus has no surface, anyone who landed on Uranus would fall down through the atmosphere, eventually reaching the liquid layer. That is, they would if they had protection from the cold and poisonous air. But by that time, they might well have been crushed by the **pressure** of the **planet's** atmosphere.

None of Uranus's **moons** seem good candidates for hosting life either. None of the moons has any atmosphere, and most are little more than balls of ice and rock. Scientists looking for signs of life in the **solar system** probably will look somewhere other than Uranus and its moons.

Highlights

- Uranus is not an inviting place for human beings or any other life forms that we know of.
- There is no oxygen to breathe in Uranus's atmosphere, and some of the planet's gases are poisonous.
- Uranus also has no solid surface.

Ariel, a moon of Uranus, in a black-and-white photo

Glossary

ammonia A compound made up of nitrogen and hydrogen.

astronomer A scientist who studies stars, planets, and other heavenly bodies.

atmosphere The gases that surround a planet.

axis In planets, the imaginary line about which the planet seems to turn, or rotate. (The axis of Earth is an imaginary line that runs from the North Pole to the South Pole.)

canyon A narrow valley with high, steep sides.

carbon A nonmetallic chemical element.

core The center part of the inside of a planet.

crater A bowl-shaped depression on the surface of a moon, planet, or asteroid.

day The time it takes a planet to rotate (spin) once around its axis and come back to the same position in relation to the sun.

density The amount of matter in a given space.

diameter The length of a straight line through the middle of a circle or a thing shaped like a ball.

elliptical Having the shape of an ellipse, which is like an oval or a flattened circle.

equator An imaginary circle around the middle of a planet.

gas giant Any of four planets—Jupiter, Saturn, Uranus, and Neptune—made up mostly of gas and liquid.

gravity The effect of a force of attraction that acts between all objects because of their mass (the amount of matter the objects have).

helium The second most abundant chemical element in the universe.

hydrogen The most abundant chemical element in the universe.

magnetic field The space around a magnet or magnetized object within which its power of attraction works.

methane A compound formed of the chemical elements carbon and hydrogen.

molten Melted.

moon A smaller body that orbits a planet.

mythology Certain types of legends or stories.

orbit The path that a smaller body takes around a larger body, such as the path that a planet takes around the sun. Also, to travel in an orbit.

organic Chemical compounds containing the element carbon.

planet A large, round body in space that orbits a star. A planet must have sufficient gravitational pull to clear other objects from the area of its orbit.

pressure The force caused by the weight of a planet's atmosphere as it presses down on the layers below it.

probe An unpiloted device sent to explore space. Most probes send data (information) from space.

rotate To spin around.

shepherd moon A moon that helps keep particles inside a planet's rings.

solar system A group of bodies in space made up of a star and the planets and other objects orbiting that star.

year The time it takes a planet to complete one orbit around the sun.

For More Information

Books

The Far Planets by Ian Graham (Smart Apple Media, 2008)

Saturn:

Destination Saturn by Giles Sparrow (PowerKids Press, 2010)

Saturn by Elaine Landau (Children's Press, 2008)

Uranus:

Uranus by Elaine Landau (Children's Press, 2008)

Uranus by Josepha Sherman (Marshall Cavendish Benchmark, 2010)

Web sites

Saturn:

NASA's Solar System Exploration: Saturn
http://sse.jpl.nasa.gov

National Geographic's Science and Space: Saturn
http://science.nationalgeographic.com

Uranus:

NASA's Solar System Exploration: Uranus
http://sse.jpl.nasa.gov

National Geographic's Science and Space: Uranus
http://science.nationalgeographic.com

Index